CINCINNATI
BENGALS HISTORY

On the front cover: Paul Brown, in his traditional hat, organized the Cincinnati Bengals in 1967. He coached the fledgling football team until 1975, but stayed involved with the orange and black until his death on August 5, 1991. (Photograph by Jack Klumpe, courtesy of Archives and Rare Books Library, University of Cincinnati.)

On the back cover: The Bengals' mascot is the Who Dey Bengal tiger. (Photograph by Frank Bodie.)

Cover background: Cincinnati plays a game against the Houston Oilers at Nippert Stadium at the University of Cincinnati. (Photograph by Jack Klumpe, courtesy of Archives and Rare Books Library, University of Cincinnati.)

CINCINNATI
BENGALS HISTORY

Christine Mersch with photographs from Jack Klumpe

ARCADIA
PUBLISHING

Published by Arcadia Publishing
Charleston SC, Chicago IL, Portsmouth NH, San Francisco CA

Printed in the United States of America

Library of Congress Catalog Card Number: 2006932962

For all general information contact Arcadia Publishing at:
Telephone 843-853-2070
Fax 843-853-0044
E-mail sales@arcadiapublishing.com
For customer service and orders:
Toll-Free 1-888-313-2665

Visit us on the Internet at www.arcadiapublishing.com

This book is dedicated to lifelong Bengals fans.

CONTENTS

ACKNOWLEDGMENTS

Sincere thanks go to Kevin Grace for helping polish this book into what it is now. Another huge thanks to the people who have donated their pictures, including Jack Klumpe, Frank Bodie, Mark Sickmiller, Bill Stoeckel, John Stanley, Bill Downs, the Edwards family, and the Boberschmidt family. Also thanks to Seth Hudson for his technical advice.

Finally I would like to thank my family and friends for supporting me during this project.

INTRODUCTION

There were three football teams in Cincinnati before the Bengals became a permanent fixture in the city. Cincinnati's first professional football team, the Cincinnati Celts, appeared on the scene in 1916 as a semiprofessional team and then turned professional in 1921. The Celts' first and only season in the American Professional Football Conference (APFC) resulted in a 1-3-0 record. All four games were played on the road, so the Celts never actually played professionally in Cincinnati. The following year, the APFC became the National Football League (NFL).

The second Cincinnati squad may be confused with the city's MLB franchise, but "Reds" was also the name of the football team in 1933. The Cincinnati Reds played for two seasons. Their first-year record was 3-6-1, and in the second season, 1934, the team lost its first eight games before folding. They played home games at Redland Field before an average of 3,000 fans.

The third team, called the Bengals, was formed in 1937. It started out as a member of the American Football League (AFL). They played at Crosley Field for an average crowd of about 8,000—much higher attendance than seen by the Celts or the Reds. This Cincinnati Bengals team had a mediocre record of 2-4-2, and the AFL went bankrupt after the 1937 season. The next year, the Bengals played 11 games as an independent squad, including three against NFL teams. Their 1938 record, 7-2-2, under head coach Dana King, included wins over the Chicago Bears (17-13) and the Pittsburgh Pirates (38-0), and a tie with the Chicago Cardinals (7-7). The next year, 1939, they joined a new version of the AFL. This year they won six games and lost only two, putting them in second place. Again this new AFL folded after only one season.

The AFL organization tried a third time to survive, in 1940, and the Bengals were again a part of it. For the next two years, 1940 and 1941, the Bengals recorded uninspiring 1-7-0 and 1-5-2 marks. They had to forfeit one game in 1940 because the team could not field all 11 positions. The AFL folded for a third time in 1941 when the United States entered World War II. This time, the Cincinnati Bengals organization went under with it. On the following pages, you will see pictures and logos of these early teams.

Professional football did not return to Cincinnati until 1967, when Paul Brown was looking to create an expansion franchise. Brown was granted his wish in yet another incarnation of the AFL, and the Cincinnati Bengals of today were born. This Bengals organization played its first game on September 6, 1968. The team played in Nippert Stadium, at the University of Cincinnati, until 1969. In 1970, the city moved its professional football team into Riverfront Stadium. In 1996, the stadium name changed to Cinergy, which is where the team remained through 1999. In 2000, the Bengals moved to their founder's namesake, the newly opened Paul Brown Stadium.

The Bengals have made two Super Bowl appearances, once in January 1982 (XVI) and once in January 1989 (XXIII). Both times they lost to the San Francisco 49ers. The Cincinnati team has played in two AFC Championship games, in the Super Bowl seasons of 1981 and 1988. They were AFC Central Division Champions five times: 1970, 1973, 1981, 1988, and 1990. During those years they also played in playoff games, as well as in 1975 and 1982 as wildcard contenders. They won the AFC North Division in 2005.

The team has hosted three hall of famers, coach Paul Brown (1968–1975), wide receiver Charlie Joiner (1972–1975), and offensive tackle Anthony Muñoz (1980–1992). Bob Johnson, who played center for the Bengals from 1968 to 1979 and was the organization's first ever draft pick, is the only Bengal player whose jersey number (No. 54) is retired. And many believe that Ken Anderson, who in 16 seasons with the Bengals passed for more total yards yet far fewer interceptions than Pittsburgh's Terry Bradshaw, belongs in Canton.

The Bengals coaches, in chronological order, are Paul Brown (1968–1975), Bill Johnson (1976–1978), Homer Rice (1978–1979), Forrest Gregg (1980–1983), Sam Wyche (1984–1991), David Shula (1992–1996), Bruce Coslet (1996–2000), Dick LeBeau (2000–2002), and Marvin Lewis (2003–present).

The team's fight song is officially called "the Bengals Growl," and the Ben-Gals cheerleaders cheer on the Bengals from the sidelines. Now there is a new generation of Bengals players and fans.

This book was written as a tribute to Cincinnati football fans and our home team, the Bengals. I hope you enjoy learning about the history of this team and recognizing key players who have made their mark on this town.

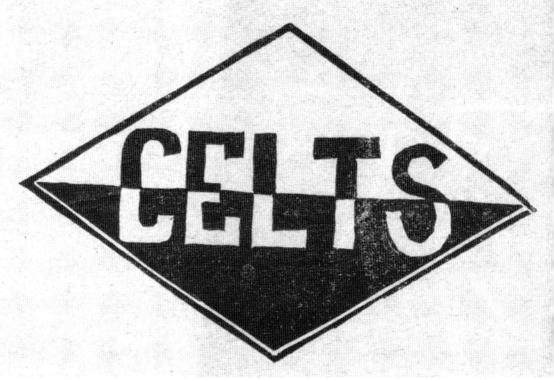

Above is the logo for the Cincinnati Celts. They had been a semiprofessional club since 1916. Outscored 117 to 14 in the 1921 season, having turned professional, the team's only two touchdowns came during a 14-0 shutout of the Muncie Flyers. The Celts also faced the defending APFC champion Akron Pros, the Cleveland Tigers (starring the legendary athlete Jim Thorpe), and the Evansville (Indiana) Crimson Giants—losing handily in each contest.

Here is a football match at Cincinnati's Redland Field in 1933. Headed by an inexperienced head coach, Al Joley, and featuring mostly rookies, the Reds were most often on the loosing end of a shutout. A mere field goal was their total offensive tally through the first six games of 1933. At 0-5-1, Joley was replaced as head coach by defensive back Mike Palm, and the Reds finished strong winning three of their last four games. But Palm was not brought back for the 1934 season, and the football team resumed its losing ways, being outscored 243 to 10 before throwing in the towel, winless, after eight games. Their final contest, a 0-64 drubbing to the Philadelphia Eagles, still stands as an NFL record for worst regular season defeat.

Goal line action is seen here at Crosley Field, home of the Cincinnati Bengals in the late 1930s and early 1940s. This earlier incarnation of the Bengals had mixed success in the on-again off-again AFL from 1937 to 1941. (Courtesy of Kevin Grace.)

Pictured, from left to right, are Ross Grant (No. 49), ? Munday (No. 43), and John Rogers (No. 38) of the Cincinnati Reds, the city's first entry to the AFL in 1933.

Jimmy Nippert never played professionally in Cincinnati. He was center for the University of Cincinnati Bearcats in the early 1920s, where he died as the result of a leg injury sustained during a 1923 contest vs. Miami University. Nippert Stadium, where the present-day Cincinnati Bengals played their first two seasons (1968 and 1969) while awaiting the completion of Riverfront Stadium, was named in his memory. (Courtesy of Kevin Grace.)

1

COACH BROWN ERA

1968–1975

Paul Brown, seen here in his usual hat and coat, would bring a smile to the faces of Cincinnati football fans in 1967 with news of the city's first professional team in over 25 years. According to the team's official Web site, he chose the Bengals name to give the team a "link with past professional football in Cincinnati." (Courtesy of Kevin Grace.)

On January 9, 1966, with city manager William Wichman acting as center and Ohio governor Jim Rhodes as quarterback, Cincinnati political and civic leaders pose at Miami Beach, Florida, seeking an NFL franchise. The background sign proclaimed, "*Our* Domed Stadium Will Be Ready: Cincinnati Wants An NFL Team." (Photograph by Jack Klumpe, courtesy of Archives and Rare Books Library, University of Cincinnati.)

With the photo opportunity over, people take down the sign, and the city awaits its new team. (Photograph by Jack Klumpe, courtesy of Archives and Rare Books Library, University of Cincinnati.)

In October 1966, football commissioner Pete Rozelle (left) and Mayor Walton Bachrach study a model of Riverfront Stadium as the city sought an NFL franchise. (Photograph by Jack Klumpe, courtesy of Archives and Rare Books Library, University of Cincinnati.)

Professional football returns to Cincinnati on September 15, 1968, as the Bengals run on to Carson Field at Nippert Stadium. The Bengals played their first regular season game in San Diego against the Chargers on September 6, 1968. Paul Robinson has the honor of being the first Bengal to score during regular-season play. He ran a 2-yard touchdown in the end zone to give Cincinnati a lead against the Chargers, but the Bengals ended up losing 13-29. At the Bengals' first regular-season home game, pictured above, they fared a bit better. They beat the Denver Broncos 24-10, in front of more than 25,000 fans. (Photograph by Jack Klumpe, courtesy of Archives and Rare Books Library, University of Cincinnati.)

This picture shows Paul Robinson with his wife and daughter. Robinson won the AFL Rookie of the Year in 1968 when he scored eight touchdowns and rushed for 1,023 yards. He also set quite a few Bengals records, including first player to rush 100 yards in a game (more than 150 yards during an Oakland Raiders game on October 27, 1968), first to rush 1,000 yards in a season (1968), and first to be selected as an All-AFL member (1968). (Photograph by Jack Klumpe, courtesy of Archives and Rare Books Library, University of Cincinnati.)

This picture was taken on September 22, 1968, in Cincinnati as the Bengals prepare to play against Buffalo. A group of Cleveland Shaker Country Club fans attending the game at Nippert Stadium wish Coach Paul Brown, who is also from Cleveland, "Good Luck" for the Bengals' inaugural season. In the picture stand Bengals players Rod Sherman (No. 23), Tom Smiley (No. 45), Howard Fest (No. 72), Pat Matson (No. 73), Bob Johnson (No. 54), and Dave Middendorf (No. 68). (Photograph by Jack Klumpe, courtesy of Archives and Rare Books Library, University of Cincinnati.)

Warren McVea (No. 42) sheds a tackler downfield during his one and only season with the Bengals, 1968. As a wide receiver, he caught two touchdowns and added another on an 80-yard run that season, before going on to play for Kansas City from 1969 through 1973. (Photograph by Jack Klumpe, courtesy of Archives and Rare Books Library, University of Cincinnati.)

COACH BROWN ERA

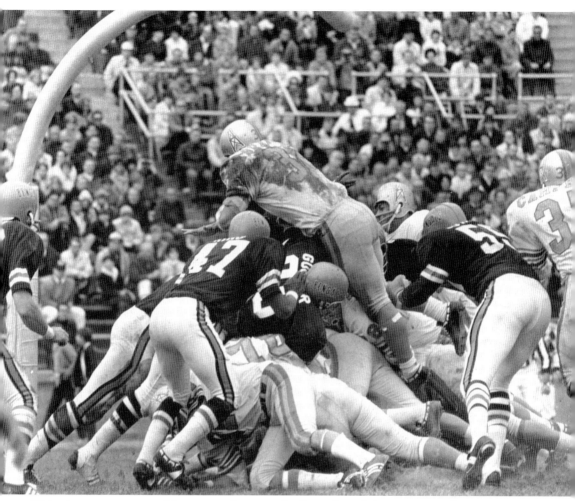

This picture captures goal line action between the Bengals and the Houston Oilers at Nippert Stadium on November 3, 1968. The Bengals lost this game, 17-27. No. 47 is Charlie King, who played for Cincinnati during the team's first two years. King was a cornerback who played for Buffalo from 1966 to 1967 before coming to Cincinnati. His hand is on Harry Gunner (in the middle of the pack), who played defensive end for the Bengals from 1968 to 1970. (Photograph by Jack Klumpe, courtesy of Archives and Rare Books Library, University of Cincinnati.)

In this picture, Pat Matson chats with Paul Brown. Matson started his NFL career playing for Denver, but when the Bengals started in 1968, he moved to Cincinnati. Matson was a Bengals offensive guard from 1968 to 1974. In 1975, he played for Green Bay before leaving the NFL after that season. (Photograph by Jack Klumpe, courtesy of Archives and Rare Books Library, University of Cincinnati.)

Here Pat Matson (No. 73) blocks Dan Birdwell of the Oakland Raiders, so that Paul Robinson (No. 18) can pick up a first down. Matson played a total of 132 games in his career, and Robinson played a total of 79. Robinson played his rookie year as a Bengal and continued to wear orange and black until 1972. After playing just four games with the Bengals during that season, he moved to the Houston Oilers team, where he played until 1973. (Photograph by Jack Klumpe, courtesy of Archives and Rare Books Library, University of Cincinnati.)

Bengals defenders are wrapping up Buffalo Bills (above) and Kansas City Chiefs (below) ball carriers. In both photographs can be seen Cincinnati safety Bobby Hunt (No. 20). He played for the black and orange in 1968 and 1969, at the end of an eight-year career in which he had 42 interceptions and one return for a touchdown. Hunt also lined up in the offensive backfield to add a rushing touchdown on a 5-yard ramble into the end zone for the Bengals in 1968. (Courtesy of Kevin Grace.)

COACH BROWN ERA

Bengal linebackers zero in on the ball carrier against the Oakland Raiders (above) and the Houston Oilers (below). Frank Buncom (No. 55) spent 1968 with Cincinnati before retiring from a seven-year career spent mostly in San Diego. Bengal defenders reach up their paws to block this Houston Oiler field-goal attempt. They lost this November 3, 1968, home game to Houston 17-27. The next year, Cincinnati returned to tie the playoff-bound Oilers 31-31 in a memorable away game before more than 45,000 people in 1969, which brought the Bengals record to 4-4-1 midseason. Linebacker Frank Buncom (No. 55), linebacker Harry Gunner (no. 89), and cornerback Bill Scott (No. 37) get air-bound to deflect the kick. That could be defensive end Marty Baccaglio (No. 85) reaching up from the center of the pack in front of Buncom and Gunner.

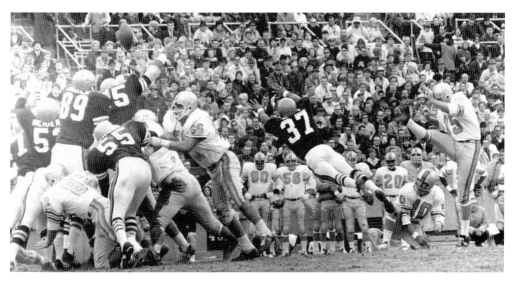

Al Beauchamp (No. 58), seen stripping the ball from an Oiler receiver, played eight strong seasons with the Bengals (1968–1975), missing only one game. He had 15 interceptions, including two

runbacks for touchdowns, and in 1970 also returned a fumble into the end zone.

Cincinnati Bengal defenders put the wraps on the Kansas City ball carrier. (Photograph by Jack Klumpe, courtesy of Archives and Rare Books Library, University of Cincinnati.)

Paul Brown watches from the sidelines during his team's inaugural NFL campaign. The Cincinnati Bengals finished the 1968 season with a record of 3-11, which put them in fifth place in the AFL West. That first Bengals team also beat the Buffalo Bills 34-23 in the beginning of the 1968 season, but out of their next 11 games, they won just once. The next year, the team won their first three games, only to end with a 4-9-1 record. Still, the quick moves of quarterback Greg Cook and linebacker Bill Bergey made others take note of the young team, and Brown was honored as Coach of the Year. (Photograph by Jack Klumpe, courtesy of Archives and Rare Books Library, University of Cincinnati.)

The Bengals begin their second season of professional football with this early quarter score in the Miami Dolphin game at Nippert Stadium, when Paul Robinson floated over the goal line for the Bengals' first touchdown of the year. The game was on September 14, 1969, and the Bengals went on to win 27-21. (Photograph by Jack Klumpe, courtesy of Archives and Rare Books Library, University of Cincinnati.)

In this picture, Bengals quarterback Sam Wyche warms up on the sidelines to go into the game for Greg Cook. This picture was taken during the Bengals vs. Denver game on December 14, 1969. Wyche was quarterback for the Bengals from 1968 to 1970, then he played for the Washington Redskins from 1971 to 1972. (Photograph by Jack Klumpe, courtesy of Archives and Rare Books Library, University of Cincinnati.)

COACH BROWN ERA

Sam Wyche (No. 14) discusses game plans with coach Paul Brown before heading onto the field. Wyche played 47 games and scored three touchdowns throughout his NFL career, playing his last two seasons with the Detroit Lions (1974) and the St. Louis Rams (1976). But the popular Bengals player also made his mark as a coach. His first coaching gig was in 1979 with then head coach Bill Walsh at the San Francisco 49ers camp. During this time, he also coached famed quarterback Joe Montana from his rookie year to his win with the 49ers against the Bengals in Super Bowl XVI. Wyche then spent some time coaching at Indiana University before moving back to Cincinnati, where he directed the Bengals from 1984 to 1991, and took them to the 1988 Super Bowl and the 1990 AFC Divisional Playoffs. He left the Bengals after the 1991 season to coach the Tampa Bay Buccaneers until 1995. (Photograph by Jack Klumpe, courtesy of Archives and Rare Books Library, University of Cincinnati.)

This picture shows quarterback Greg Cook on the left, and an unknown player on the right. Cook played football at the University of Cincinnati before joining the Bengals as the first-round draft pick in 1969. He suffered a career-ending shoulder injury during the next year's training camp and was replaced by Virgil Carter. Cook did play one more game with the Bengals in 1973 and left the organization in 1974. (Photograph by Jack Klumpe, courtesy of Archives and Rare Books Library, University of Cincinnati.)

Bengals quarterback Virgil Carter talks with Greg Cook. As this picture shows, Cook's shoulder is in a sling. During Cook's rookie NFL season, 1969, he won Rookie of the Year. His honors include the AFL passing title after he ended the season passing for 1,854 yards, and the Bengals' title of having an average yardage gain of 9.41 per passing attempt. (Photograph by Jack Klumpe, courtesy of Archives and Rare Books Library, University of Cincinnati.)

COACH BROWN ERA

Here Paul Brown stands with Virgil Carter and Carter's wife. Carter was the quarterback for the Bengals from 1970 to 1973, and played for both San Diego and Chicago, too. Previous Cincinnati winners of this trophy were running back Paul Robinson (No. 18), quarterback Greg Cook (No. 12), and Bill Bergey (No. 66). Bergey played with the Bengals from 1969 to 1973 as a linebacker. (Photograph by Jack Klumpe, courtesy of Archives and Rare Books Library, University of Cincinnati.)

The Bengal equipment manager does his part to ready the team for its Sunday afternoon appointments. (Photograph by Jack Klumpe, courtesy of Archives and Rare Books Library, University of Cincinnati.)

Paul Brown is seen here with hands on hips, assessing the team's talent at their Wilmington College training camp. Behind the coach are running back Ron Lamb (No. 40), who played with Cincinnati from 1968 to 1971, and longtime Bengal center Bob Johnson (No. 54). Johnson made the Pro Bowl as a rookie. (Photograph by Jack Klumpe, courtesy of Archives and Rare Books Library, University of Cincinnati.)

While the Bengals were improving on the field at Nippert Stadium in 1968 and 1969, a new home was nearing completion along the Ohio River. Riverfront is seen here under construction from without (above) and from within (below). (Photograph above by Jack Klumpe, courtesy of Archives and Rare Books Library, University of Cincinnati.)

As opening day 1970 approaches, the Cincinnati skyline looms above a completed Riverfront Stadium. (Photograph by Jack Klumpe, courtesy of Archives and Rare Books Library,

Snow-covered seats await the city's football fans for the Bengals' next home game. (Photograph by Jack Klumpe, courtesy of Archives and Rare Books Library, University of Cincinnati.)

COACH BROWN ERA

University of Cincinnati.)

Motorists had to access this small, dead-end street near the stadium for free parking. (Photograph by Jack Klumpe, courtesy of Archives and Rare Books Library, University of Cincinnati.)

New Astroturf is being installed to the playing field under the lights at Riverfront stadium. The Cincinnati Bengals played their inaugural game at Riverfront on September 20, 1970, a 31-21 victory against the Oakland Raiders before 56,616 fans. The team lost their next six games but went on to win their final seven games for an 8-6 record and the team's first birth in the NFL playoffs. They were 5-2 at their new home this first year at Riverfront. (Photographs by Jack Klumpe, courtesy of Archives and Rare Books Library, University of Cincinnati.)

COACH BROWN ERA

Pictured here in 1970 is the Brown family, from left to right, Mike, father Paul, Pete, and Robin. Mike took over responsibilities for team ownership after his father's death in 1991. (Photograph by Jack Klumpe, courtesy of Archives and Rare Books Library, University of Cincinnati.)

New Bengal quarterback Ken Anderson (left) poses with coach Paul Brown and quarterbacks/receivers coach Bill Walsh. Anderson was picked 67th overall in the 1971 NFL draft and played his entire career—16 seasons—in the Bengal uniform. He set numerous team and league records, played in four NFL Pro Bowls, and was awarded the 1981 NFL Most Valuable Player (MVP) for leading Cincinnati to Super Bowl XVI. Walsh stayed with the Bengals through the 1975 season. He later brought this offensive style to the San Francisco 49ers when he was hired as head coach 1979–1988. He led the 49ers to three Super Bowl victories, including the 26-21 win over Anderson and the 1981 Bengals. (Photograph by Jack Klumpe, courtesy of Archives and Rare Books Library, University of Cincinnati.)

Oilers ball carrier Hoyle Granger climbs over the top to gain 3 yards for a touchdown against the Bengals. At this November 3, 1968, game, the Bengals lost a close game to the Oilers, 17-27. (Photograph by Jack Klumpe, courtesy of Archives and Rare Books Library, University of Cincinnati.)

Broncos running back Garret Ford is smothered by Bengal defenders as he tries to run around his right side. That is defensive end Dennis Randall trying to strip the ball. This September 15, 1968, game at Nippert Stadium resulted in a home game win 24-10. (Photograph by Jack Klumpe, courtesy of Archives and Rare Books Library, University of Cincinnati.)

Tom Smiley (No. 45) is greatly annoyed at Bronco Richard Jackson's method of tackling, as he grabs at the jersey of the Bengal running back (above). In an early Bengals vs. Dolphins game, Tom Smiley falls forward for a few extra yards as the Miami defender loses his helmet (below). Smiley played in 1968 for Cincinnati during his brief, three-year AFL/NFL career, scoring one touchdown as a Bengal. He ended his career with Denver in 1969 and Houston in 1970. (Photographs by Jack Klumpe, courtesy of Archives and Rare Books Library, University of Cincinnati.)

Dan Middendorf, the Bengals player on the ground, throws his block at Frank Richter too soon, but Essex Johnson (No. 19) leaps over his teammate and scampers 44 yards for a Bengal touchdown. Johnson played for the orange and black the entire Paul Brown era, 1968 through 1975, before one final season in Tampa Bay. His best year was 1973, rushing for 997 yards and scoring seven touchdowns. (Photograph by Jack Klumpe, courtesy of Archives and Rare Books Library, University of Cincinnati.)

Bill Bergey tackles Wendell Hayes too late to keep him from scoring for the Kansas City Chiefs. Bergey played for the Bengals from 1969 to 1973, before ending a solid 12-year career as a linebacker for several seasons with the Philadelphia Eagles. (Photograph by Jack Klumpe, courtesy of Archives and Rare Books Library, University of Cincinnati.)

Virgil Carter, the Bengals quarterback from 1970 to 1973, sits on the sidelines during a game. Carter (No. 11) threw for 22 touchdowns and had four rushing touchdowns while with the Bengals. In 2006, the Bengals continue to play in the AFC division. (Photograph by Jack Klumpe, courtesy of Archives and Rare Books Library, University of Cincinnati.)

This picture shows Paul Brown with his other coaches. In 1970, the AFL and NFL merged. This meant the relatively young Cincinnati Bengals had to play against the Cleveland Browns, and the two teams have since remained rivals. It was during 1970 that Cincinnati opened Riverfront Stadium, which would be the Bengals' home on the Ohio River for the next 30 years, even after a name change to Cinergy. (Photograph by Jack Klumpe, courtesy of Archives and Rare Books Library, University of Cincinnati.)

COACH BROWN ERA

In this 1970s-era picture are, from left to right, Pete Rozell, Pete Brown, Wally Powers, and John Murdough. In 1970, the Bengals won their first home game, 31-21, against the Oakland Raiders. Their second game against the Detroit Lions, which the Bengals lost 3-38, started a six-game losing streak. True to Bengals style, the 1970 team turned around their losing streak during a game against the Buffalo Bills, in which they won 43-14. The Bengals ended the season with an 8-6 record, which won them first place in the AFC Central division. For their first playoff game, they faced the Baltimore Colts. The Bengals, unfortunately, could not keep their winning streak going, as they lost 0-17 at Memorial Stadium in Baltimore. (Photograph by Jack Klumpe, courtesy of Archives and Rare Books Library, University of Cincinnati.)

In 1972, with Ken Anderson as starting quarterback, the Bengals won four of their first five games, but at the end of the season they had a record of 8-6. Anderson really hit his stride the next year, in 1973, with a 2,428-yard passing record. He also threw 18 touchdown passes, giving the Bengals a spectacular record of 10-4. The Bengals won the last six games of the season. Anderson was drafted by the Bengals in the third round of the 1971 draft, and he continued to play for the team until 1986. During that time, he scored four invites to the Pro Bowl (1975, 1976, 1981, and 1982) and was responsible for more than 200 touchdowns. Another exciting home game was on January 10, 1982. The Bengals challenged the San Diego Chargers during a winter chill, with the temperature at 59 degrees below 0. The home team pulled off a win, 27-7, and headed to their first ever Super Bowl. (Photograph by Jack Klumpe, courtesy of Archives and Rare Books Library, University of Cincinnati.)

COACH BROWN ERA

This picture shows Pittsburgh Steeler Preston Pearson (No. 26) after he receives a pitch out from quarterback Terry Bradshaw (No. 12). The Bengals' Ken Avery (No. 51) is on the ground. Avery was a linebacker with the Bengals from 1969 to 1974 in the middle of a nine-year professional football career. (Photograph by Jack Klumpe, courtesy of Archives and Rare Books Library, University of Cincinnati.)

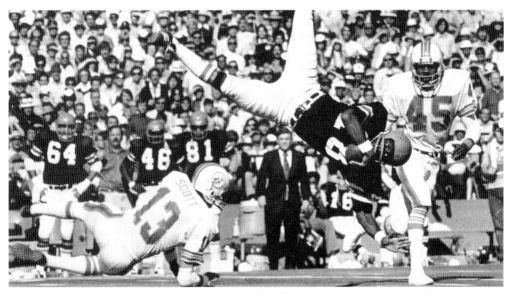

This picture was taken at the AFC divisional playoff game on December 23, 1973. During the 1973 season, the Bengals won the AFC Central Division title for the second time (the first was during the 1970 season). They went on to play the Miami Dolphins, the defending Super Bowl champions, in the AFC divisional playoffs. The first half of the game the Bengals kept the score at 16-21, but the Dolphins won the game 16-34. (Photograph by Jack Klumpe, courtesy of Archives and Rare Books Library, University of Cincinnati.)

This picture shows Mike Reid (No. 74) running onto the field in the opening game of an early 1970s season. The rest of the Bengals are waiting for their names to be called over the public-address system. Reid was a six-foot-three-inch defensive tackle at Penn State until he graduated in 1969. He played the same position for the Bengals from 1970 to 1974. He went to the Pro Bowl in 1972 and 1973 but left the NFL after the 1974 season to be a music composer. (Photograph by Jack Klumpe, courtesy of Archives and Rare Books Library, University of Cincinnati.)

This picture shows Mike Reid on crutches for a Bengals exhibition game after suffering a knee injury. (Photograph by Jack Klumpe, courtesy of Archives and Rare Books Library, University of Cincinnati.)

COACH BROWN ERA

Here Mike Reid plays the piano with the Riverfront Stadium in the background. Reid studied piano at Penn State, and after his NFL career, composed songs for Willie Nelson, Ronnie Milsap, Kenny Rogers, Tim McGraw, Bette Midler, Wynonna Judd, and Bonnie Raitt. He also writes classical music, including pieces like *Prairie Songs*, *Tales of Appalachia*, and *Different Fields*—a one-act opera. He has also written musicals such as *The Ballad of Little Jo* and *Shane*. He is a Grammy-winning songwriter. (Photograph by Jack Klumpe, courtesy of Archives and Rare Books Library, University of Cincinnati.)

Paul Brown kneels with assistant coach Bill Johnson. Johnson worked as an assistant coach from 1968 to 1975 and replaced Brown as the Bengals coach in 1976. (Photograph by Jack Klumpe, courtesy of Archives and Rare Books Library, University of Cincinnati.)

Here Paul Brown stands with other Bengals players. At the end of the 1975 season, Paul Brown stepped back from coaching to focus on his role as general manager. He was named Hall of Fame Coach in 1967 for his coaching history with the Cleveland Browns, a team he organized in 1946. During his time with the Browns, he racked up a 167-53-8 record plus four AAFC titles. Brown was responsible for one losing season during his 17-year tenure at Cleveland. Born on September 7, 1908, in Norwalk, Ohio, his full name was Paul Eugene Brown. (Photograph by Jack Klumpe, courtesy of Archives and Rare Books Library, University of Cincinnati.)

COACH BROWN ERA

2

THE SECOND GENERATION

1976–1989

The Bengals' new head coach Bill Johnson would have plenty to grimace about over the next few seasons. Johnson resigned during the 1978 season after the Bengals lost their first five games. He was replaced by Homer Rice midseason, who helped the Bengals win four games. Johnson returned to the Bengals during 1985–1990 to work as an assistant coach. (Photograph by Jack Klumpe, courtesy of Archives and Rare Books Library, University of Cincinnati.)

THE SECOND GENERATION

Bengals player Bob Trumpy (No. 84) is tackled during a game against the New England Patriots. Trumpy's introduction to the NFL was during the Bengals inaugural season. He continued as a tight end with the Bengals until he retired in 1977. The Bengals had a mediocre 7-7 record in 1974, but quarterback Ken Anderson had another stellar season in 1975, passing for 3,169 yards. The team won the first six games of the season. Week seven they lost to defending Super Bowl champion Pittsburgh Steelers 24-30. The Bengals bounced back to finish with an 11-3 record, which qualified them for the AFC Central Wild Card playoffs. The Bengals played the Oakland Raiders in the Divisional Playoffs. Although the Bengals scored an exciting two late-quarter touchdowns, it was not enough to beat the Raiders, and the final score was 28-31. In 1976, running back Archie Griffin came on the scene. Griffin won the Heisman twice at Ohio State University, and rushed for 625 yards during his rookie year at Cincinnati. (Photograph by Jack Klumpe, courtesy of Archives and Rare Books Library, University of Cincinnati.)

Here is a picture of Archie Griffin, No. 45 on the Bengals. Griffin played college ball at Ohio State University, where he was an All-American and won two Heisman trophies (1974 and 1975). He was a running back for the Bengals from 1976 to 1983. He has been inducted to the National Football Foundation, Rose Bowl, Ohio State University Athletics, and National High School Halls of Fame. (Photograph by Jack Klumpe, courtesy of Archives and Rare Books Library, University of Cincinnati.)

In November 1977, the Bengals played this game in the snow. The Bengals ended the 1977 season with an 8-6 record. They won against the Seattle Seahawks, Green Bay Packers, Miami Dolphins, New York Giants, and the Kansas City Chiefs. They split games with the Cleveland Browns, the Pittsburgh Steelers, and the Houston Oilers. (Courtesy of the Jack Klumpe collection.)

This picture, taken on December 18, 1977, shows the Bengals playing at the Houston Astrodome. The Bengals lost this game to the Oilers, 16-21. Due to this loss, the Bengals could not proceed to the playoffs. But that did not stop some Bengals players from heading to the Pro Bowl, including defensive end Coy Bacon (No. 79), safety Tommy Casanova (No. 37) and cornerback Lemar Parrish (No. 20). (Photograph by Jack Klumpe, courtesy of Archives and Rare Books Library, University of Cincinnati.)

This picture shows the two Bahr brothers. Chris Bahr (No. 10) was drafted by the Bengals in 1976 and continued to be their kicker from 1976 to 1979. After playing with the Bengals, he went on to play for the Raiders (both at Oakland from 1980 to 1981 and at Los Angeles from 1982 to 1988) and the San Diego Chargers. He left the NFL in 1989. Brother Matt Bahr was also a NFL kicker from 1979 to 1995. (Photograph by Jack Klumpe, courtesy of Archives and Rare Books Library, University of Cincinnati.)

THE SECOND GENERATION

Anthony Muñoz shows off for the cameras. In 1980, Anthony Muñoz was the Bengals' first-round draft pick. He played offensive tackle for the Bengals until 1992, and he was a part of the Bengals team when they went to the Super Bowl in 1982 and 1989. He was named All-Pro 11 times and went to the Pro Bowl 11 times, both consecutively, and has been named the NFL Offensive Lineman of the Year three times and NFL Players Association Lineman of the Year four times. He was inducted to the Pro Football Hall of Fame in 1998, making history as the first Latino to do so. Muñoz is a class act on and off the field; his Anthony Muñoz Foundation helps support children throughout the Ohio, Kentucky, and Indiana region. The foundation started on April 17, 2002, and has since impacted innumerable youths in the area. (Photograph by Jack Klumpe, courtesy of Archives and Rare Books Library, University of Cincinnati.)

This picture shows Bengals coach Forest Gregg, who led the Bengals team from 1980 to 1983. Homer Rice, the previous coach, lasted until the end of the 1979 season, but the team continued their losing streak, ending with a 4-12 record that year. Rice was fired after his first full season as coach, and Forrest Gregg was hired to replace him. During Gregg's coaching reign, the Bengals posted a 6-10 record in 1980, a 12-4 record in 1981, a 7-2 record in 1982 (because of a players' strike), and a 7-9 record in 1983. In 1985, Boomer Esiason became the lead quarterback, and wide receiver Eddie Brown won the 1985 Rookie of the Year. In 1986, Esiason passed for 3,959 yards, helping the Bengals keep a 10-6 record. A strike kept the main Bengals players out of commission from September 22 to October 15, 1987, and they ended that year with a 4-11 record. (Photograph by Jack Klumpe, courtesy of Archives and Rare Books Library, University of Cincinnati.)

THE SECOND GENERATION

This picture shows coach Forest Gregg, who coached the Bengals to their first Super Bowl in 1981. At the start of that season, the Bengals won three of their first four games, leading to an AFC Central title. At Super Bowl XVI, the Bengals went up against the San Francisco 49ers. The bowl was played in Pontiac, Michigan. The Bengals lost a close game to the 49ers, 21-26, and managed to rack up more yards than San Francisco (356-275). This was the first time in Super Bowl history this happened. (Photograph by Jack Klumpe, courtesy of Archives and Rare Books Library, University of Cincinnati.)

Gregg's third coaching season was marked by a two-month player strike, where the regular Bengals players missed eight regular-season games. They finished the season 7-2, which made them the third seed in the eight-team AFC playoff. In 1983, the Bengals lost six of their first seven games but continued to win six more games throughout the season, leaving them with a 7-9 record. Gregg left after the 1983 season. (Photograph by Jack Klumpe, courtesy of Archives and Rare Books Library, University of Cincinnati.)

Ken Anderson, the Bengals' quarterback from 1971 to 1986, won the 1981 NFL MVP, leading the Bengals to a 12-4 record. Anderson also won the Offensive Player of the Year because he passed for 3,754 yards and threw 29 touchdown passes. This exceptional season, which is also known for being the Bengals' best road record (6-2), led to the first ever playoff game at Riverfront Stadium. The Bengals played the Buffalo Bills in an exciting touch-and-go game. Late in the fourth quarter, the score was tied at 21. Anderson threw a 16-yard touchdown to Cris Collinsworth, which helped the Bengals advance to the AFC championship game. (Photograph by Jack Klumpe, courtesy of Archives and Rare Books Library, University of Cincinnati.)

THE SECOND GENERATION

Rookie wide receiver Cris Collinsworth was another star in 1981. He caught eight of Anderson's touchdown passes and gained 1,009 receiving yards. He also won a trip to the Pro Bowl. Collinsworth played with the Bengals until 1988, scoring a career total of 36 touchdowns and attending three consecutive Pro Bowls (1981–1983). He now works as a writer and broadcaster and has won two Emmys for his work. (Courtesy of Kevin Grace.)

Ken Anderson throws a pass in practice. In 1971, Anderson was drafted by the Bengals in the third round. He became the team's starting quarterback the next year, taking over for Virgil Carter. Through his 16-year career he won numerous accolades, including the NFL passing championship in 1974 and 1975. (Photograph by Jack Klumpe, courtesy of Archives and Rare Books Library, University of Cincinnati.)

Jack Thompson, a Bengals quarterback who played with Ken Anderson, signs an autograph for a young fan. Thompson played from 1979 to 1982 and was nicknamed "the Throwin' Samoan." Thompson graduated from Washington State and was recruited by the Bengals in the first round of the draft. At the start of his rookie season, the Bengals lost their first six games but won a surprising home game against the Pittsburgh Steelers 34-10. Despite this loss, the Steelers went on to win their fourth Super Bowl in six years. The Bengals again won against the Steelers in 1980, who, because of the loss, were denied another shot at the Super Bowl. In 1984, the Bengals lost their first five games but were able to get it together in the end, finishing with an 8-8 record. During Thompson's Bengal career, he was responsible for almost 20 touchdowns. (Photograph by Jack Klumpe, courtesy of Archives and Rare Books Library, University of Cincinnati.)

This picture was taken of then Bengals quarterback Sam Wyche (No. 14) being tackled by a Houston Oilers player. Wyche coached the Bengals during their second-greatest season in 1988. After racking up a 12-4 regular-season record, the Bengals easily beat the Seattle Seahawks 21-13 in the first-round AFC Divisional Playoffs. Next the team won the AFC championship game against the Buffalo Bills 21-10. Super Bowl XXIII again pitted the Bengals against the San Francisco 49ers. At halftime, the score remained tied at 3. This marked the first time a Super

THE SECOND GENERATION

Bowl was ever tied at halftime, and the game became even tenser through the next two quarters. Cincinnati took the lead toward the end, at 16-13. But with just 3 minutes 20 seconds left in the fourth quarter, Joe Montana, legendary 49ers quarterback, led his team to the Bengals' 10-yard line, which put them in place to score. Montana threw to wide receiver John Taylor, who scored with 34 seconds left to secure the 49ers win. The end score was 16-20. (Photograph by Jack Klumpe, courtesy of Archives and Rare Books Library, University of Cincinnati.)

Pat McInally (No. 87) was a wide receiver for the Bengals from 1976 to 1985. He attended Harvard College, where he played wide receiver. In fact, he is the only Harvard graduate to have played both in a Pro Bowl and a Super Bowl. Upon graduation in 1975, he was drafted by the Bengals in the fifth round on the injured reserve list, since he had recently broken his fibula during a college All-Star Game against the Pittsburgh Steelers. His leg healed, and he continued to play for the Bengals for 10 seasons. After the NFL, he wrote the book *Moms and Dads, Kids and Sports*, and also spent some time as a syndicated newspaper columnist, where he wrote the column "Pat Answers for Kids." He was inducted to the Harvard University Hall of Fame in 1997 and founded the Good Sports for Life organization, which encourages sportsmanship among youth sports. During his last two years with the Bengals, McInally played with Boomer Esiason, the Bengals' starting quarterback. Esiason quickly racked up the statistics his second season, passing for 3,443 yards and throwing 27 touchdown passes. The team finished with a 7-9 record in 1985. (Photograph by Jack Klumpe, courtesy of Archives and Rare Books Library, University of Cincinnati.)

THE SECOND GENERATION

3

INTO A NEW HOME

1990 – 2005

The Bengals current field prominently displays the leaping Bengal tiger logo at its center. The fierce image contradicts a struggling decade of the 1990s during the team's final years at Riverfront Stadium. The team posted a 52-108 record for the 1990s. A 9-7 record in 1990 put them first in the AFC Central and gave them a wild card entrance to the playoffs. They beat the Houston Oilers 41-14. For their next game in the divisional round, the Bengals played the Los Angeles Raiders in Los Angeles. Unfortunately the Bengals suffered a 10-20 loss. After Paul Brown's death in 1991 at 82, his son, Mike Brown, took over as leader of the Bengals franchise. Unfortunately the older Brown's death seemed to take a toll on the team, and the Bengals lost their first eight games in 1991, finishing with a 3-13 record. After the season, coach Sam Wyche left and Dave Shula was hired. (Photograph by Frank Bodie.)

This picture shows the present-day Bengals home, Paul Brown Stadium, built in 2000. Cincinnati taxpayers approved a half-cent-per-dollar sales tax increase in March 1996 to start construction on both the Great American Ball Park and Paul Brown Stadium. Cincinnatians broke ground on Paul Brown Stadium on April 25, 1998, and the stadium was opened for football games in 2000. The stadium can hold up to 65,328 fans and sits on approximately 22 acres of land. The building is 157 feet high. The stadium has been recognized by *Architectural Record* and *Architecture*, two national architecture magazines, for its creative design. (Photograph by Frank Bodie.)

INTO A NEW HOME

Another picture of the imposing Paul Brown Stadium belies the team's struggles during the 1990s. Bengals quarterback Dave Klinger started the 1992 season, but the team ended with a 5-11 record and lost offensive tackle Anthony Muñoz when he retired at the end of the season. In 1993, the team lost their first 10 games before beating the Los Angeles Raiders 16-10 at home. The Bengals won two more games at the end of the season, giving them their second 3-13 season in three years. In 1994, Dave Shula and the Bengals played his father's team, the Miami Dolphins, making it the first ever NFL father-son coaching match up. Played on October 2 at Riverfront Stadium, the Dolphins won 23-7. The Bengals posted their third 3-13 season within four years, and Klinger was replaced by Jeff Blake. In 1995, Blake threw the Bengals to a 2-0 start in the beginning of the season, but it was not enough to lift them out of their slump. The Cincinnati team finished 7-9. (Photograph by Frank Bodie.)

This is a picture of Paul Brown Stadium, as seen from across the river. At the beginning of 1996, the Bengals organization struggled, losing six of their first seven games. Former Bengals tight end Bruce Coslet replaced Dave Shula as coach and turned the team around. The Cincinnati Bengals won their first three games under his new coaching style, ending the 1996 season with an 8-8 record. The beginning of 1997 started off on the right foot, as the Bengals won the first game of the season. But after this impressive showing, the Bengals lost their next seven games. This not only dashed their playoff hopes, but it also cost Jeff Blake his starting quarterback job. They played better in the last half of this season, with rookie Corey Dillon rushing for an impressive 1,129 yards. The team's 1998 season was the fourth time they posted a 3-13 record, and 1999 brought worse luck. They lost 10 of their first 11 games and won two more games before facing the Cleveland Browns at home, where the Bengals won 44-28. Still, they ended the 1999 season with a 4-12 record. (Photograph by Frank Bodie.)

INTO A NEW HOME

Before Paul Brown Stadium was built, the Bengals played in Cinergy Field with the Cincinnati Reds baseball team. On September 9, 1996, the stadium was officially named Cinergy Field after the naming rights were sold to the electric utility company for $6 million. On August 1, 2000, workers began to demolish parts of the stadium, including the left- and center-field stands. The stadium seats, all 2,500 of them, had been auctioned off on June 10, 2000. (Photograph by Jack Klumpe, courtesy of Archives and Rare Books Library, University of Cincinnati.)

On Sunday, December 29, 2002, at 8:00 a.m., Cinergy Field was imploded. Many fans gathered on the banks of the Ohio River to watch the 32-year-old field be demolished. The implosion was also shown on local television stations, and many Internet sites streamed the view online. (Photographs by Frank Bodie.)

INTO A NEW HOME

More than 1,200 pounds of dynamite and nitroglycerine were used to implode the building, section by section. O'Rourke Wrecking Company was tapped to oversee the demolition and have the site cleaned up by August 31. (Photographs by Frank Bodie.)

Some memorable Riverfront/Cinergy moments include the first Bengals game at the stadium when they played the Oakland Raiders on September 20, 1970, and won 31-21. On November 15 of that same year, the Bengals beat the Cleveland Browns. This victory marked Paul Brown's first over his former franchise. Another memorable moment happened on December 10, 1989, when the Bengals lost to the Seattle Seahawks. It was a snowy day, and the people seated in the stadium began to throw snowballs onto the field. Sam Wyche, the Bengals coach at that time, used the on-field microphone to plead with fans to stop by yelling, "You don't live in Cleveland, you live in Cincinnati!" And who could forget the Browns vs. Bengals match-up on December 21, 1980, when receiver Pat McInally was knocked unconscious by Browns safety Thom Darden, carried off the field via a stretcher, but later returned to catch a 59-yard touchdown pass. The Bengals played their last game in the Cinergy stadium on December 12, 1999, against the Cleveland Browns, which they won 44-28. (Photograph by Frank Bodie.)

INTO A NEW HOME

Huge clouds of dust surround the implosion site, as spectators continue to watch. The United Way sponsored a raffle to pick the one person who would push the ceremonial button to bring down the Cinergy stadium. Jim Matthews won the lottery. Matthews, who was 38 years old at the time, used to live in Sharonville but had since moved to Dallas, Texas. He beat out more than 2,000 other competitors for the opportunity. All in all, the United Way raised more than $20,000 in the raffle. (Photograph by Frank Bodie.)

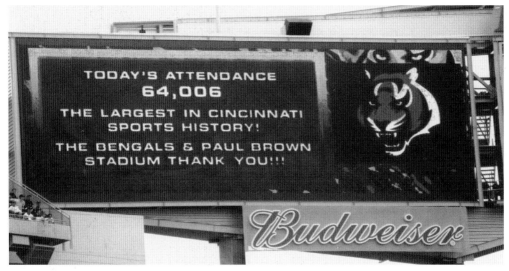

The scoreboard welcomes fans into the Bengals first regular season game played at Paul Brown Stadium, against the Cleveland Browns, on September 10, 2000. The legendary Bengals vs. Browns game drew an unprecedented amount of people to the stadium. Unfortunately the Bengals lost this game 7-24. The team was shutout in their next two games, and coach Bruce Coslet resigned. Coach Dick LeBeau was hired, but the Bengals continued to lose, ending the season with a 4-12 record. (Photograph by Frank Bodie.)

In the center of this picture stands Scott Rehberg (No. 79). Rehberg played college football at Central Michigan and was drafted by the New England Patriots in 1997. He played for the Patriots until 1998, and played for the Cleveland Browns in 1999. In 2000, he was picked up by the Cincinnati Bengals, where he played through the 2003 season. Also in this picture is Rich Branham (No. 74). (Photograph by Frank Bodie.)

INTO A NEW HOME

Peter Warrick (No. 80) was recruited to be a wide receiver for the Cincinnati Bengals in 2000. At 5 feet 11 inches and 192 pounds, Warrick scored 18 receiving touchdowns, two rushing touchdowns, and two touchdowns off punt returns while he was with the Bengals. He played at Florida State before heading into the NFL, and he currently plays for the Seattle Seahawks. (Photograph by Frank Bodie.)

Warrick is also remembered for scoring the first Bengals points in Paul Brown Stadium. In 2001, the team's hopes soared with a new quarterback, Jon Kitna, who had played for the Seattle Seahawks. The team won their first two games and posted a winning record of 4-3 in the first half of the season. (Photograph by Frank Bodie.)

Akili Smith (No. 11) prepares to throw long in a game against the Cleveland Browns. The new stadium did not change the team's luck; the Bengals started the 2000 season with a six-game losing streak. But on October 22, 2000, their luck changed. The Bengals beat the Denver Broncos at the Paul Brown Stadium 31-21. The next week, they also beat the Browns at Cleveland 12-3. The rest of the season, however, was a struggle. The Bengals ended with a 4-12 record. Coach Bruce Coslet had resigned on September 25, 2000, and was replaced by assistant head coach Dick

INTO A NEW HOME

LeBeau. The 2001 season ended with a 6-10 record, and the Bengals set a new franchise record for losses in 2002, as they finished the season with a 2-14 record. This prompted an organizational overhaul in 2003. Coach Dick LeBeau was not retained for the next season, and Akili Smith was released. The two former Bengals were replaced with coach Marvin Lewis and quarterback Carson Palmer, who had won the 2002 Heisman Trophy while at the University of Southern California. Palmer was the top overall pick in the NFL draft. (Photograph by Frank Bodie.)

The Bengals tiger growls at opponents on the new basketball court built inside the Bengals' locker room. The weight room and other rooms inside the Bengals' lair were remodeled in early 2003. According to a *Cincinnati Enquirer* article, the new and improved workout areas have seen an increase in attendance from Bengals players. (Photograph by Frank Bodie.)

The double spas await tired Bengal players after a game. Ray Oliver is the assistant strength and conditioning coach for the Bengals. Oliver played football at the Ohio State University from 1980 to 1981 and has worked as a strength and training coach for both football and basketball programs for more than 20 years. He signed on with the Bengals in 2004. (Photograph by Frank Bodie.)

Weights and more workout equipment sit and wait to help the new Bengals team beef up for games. This weight room was part of a $250,000 renovation. Chip Morton is the strength and conditioning coach for the Bengals. Morton's first job as an assistant strength and conditioning coach was with the Ohio State University from 1985 to 1986, and from 1987 to 1991 he worked the same job at Penn State. The new spas, basketball court, and weight rooms are not the only new items the Bengals can brag about. They also had a new, updated video department installed, which will allow them to be better prepared on each game day. The team also established a distinct, official off-season conditioning program. (Photograph by Frank Bodie.)

Corey Dillon (No. 28) runs onto the field. Dillon was drafted by the Bengals in 1997 and worked as a running back through the 2003 season. On December 4, 1997, as a rookie, Dillon ran for 246 yards in a game against the Tennessee Titans. This run broke Jim Brown's NFL rookie rushing record. In 1998, Corey Dillon made more headlines by rushing for 1,130 yards. In 2000, he rushed for 278 yards in a single-game, breaking a record held by Walter Payton since 1977. Dillon set more records over the course of the 2000 season by rushing for 1,435 yards, and he rushed for 1,315 yards in 2001. In 2004, the Bengals traded Dillon to the New England Patriots, promoting Rudi Johnson to starting running back. Dillon and the Patriots went on to win the 2004 and 2005 Super Bowls. (Photograph by Frank Bodie.)

Carson Palmer warms up at the 2003 home game against the Ravens. Marvin Lewis became the Bengals' coach on January 14, 2003, and eventually led the team to its first playoff game in 15 years (the 2005 season). In 2006, Lewis signed on to be the team's leader through the 2010 season. (Photograph by Frank Bodie.)

The Ben-Gals root for their home team as they wait for the rest of the Bengals players to come out. The Bengals won this October 19, 2003, game 34-26 but lost the December 7, 2003, away game at Baltimore (13-31). Because of the team's improved record, Coach Lewis placed second in the Associated Press' NFL Coach of the Year poll. Instead, Patriots coach Bill Belichick won. (Photograph by Frank Bodie.)

This picture shows the opening events at the start of the 2003 home Bengals vs. Browns game. Corey Dillon runs out through the line of Ben-Gals and smoke from fireworks. The Bengals maintained an even record for the 2003 season, 8-8-0. This December 28th game, however, the Bengals lost 14-22. (Photograph by Frank Bodie.)

Jon Kitna (No. 3) runs out onto the field at the start of the 2003 Bengals vs. Browns home game. Kitna was the starting quarterback for the Bengals at this time, and he threw for 3,591 yards and 26 touchdowns this season. Other 2003 season leaders included Rudi Johnson for his rushing statistics, Chad Johnson as a receiver, and Shayne Graham for scoring 106 points. (Photograph by Frank Bodie.)

INTO A NEW HOME

In 2001, Chad Johnson (No. 85) suffered a broken clavicle, but returned to active duty by the end of the season. But in the 2002 season, Johnson played in every regular season game for the first time, breaking many Bengals franchise records. He posted 1,166 receiving yards, making him the only first- or second-year Bengal to do so. He had five 100-yard receiving games, including three straight—November 10 against the Baltimore Ravens, November 17 against the Cleveland Browns, and November 24 against the Pittsburgh Steelers. Johnson grew up in Miami, Florida, went to Miami Beach High School, and majored in physical education at Oregon State. During his 2000 college season, he averaged 21.8 yards per catch and helped his team win the Fiesta Bowl over Notre Dame. While at Oregon State, Johnson also played with T. J. Houshmandzadeh, who would eventually become Johnson's Bengals teammate. (Photograph by Frank Bodie.)

Here Jon Kitna (No. 3) walks across the field during the 2003 Bengals vs. Browns home game. Born on September 21, 1972, Kitna went to college at Central Washington and went to work for the Seattle Seahawks in 1997. He played there until 2001, when he was drafted by the Bengals as their starting quarterback. (Photograph by Frank Bodie.)

In this huddle, during the 2003 Bengals vs. Browns home game, both Chad Johnson (No. 85) and Rudi Johnson (No. 32) are visible. Kitna is in the middle of the pack. Chad went on to play in the 2003 Pro Bowl, as did Willie Anderson (No. 71). Before the 2003 season started, the Bengals picked up quarterback Carson Palmer, who did not play as a rookie but would become the Bengals' starting quarterback the next year. (Photograph by Frank Bodie.)

INTO A NEW HOME

During the 2003 Bengals vs. Browns home game, Kitna (No. 3) prepares to make a play for the end zone. Although the Bengals lost this game, they had won against the Browns previously in the season, 21-14. Head coach Marvin Lewis was hired on January 14, 2003, to be the ninth head coach of the Bengals. (Photograph by Frank Bodie.)

Taken at the Bengals vs. 49ers game on December 14, 2003, this picture shows the fireworks that ushered in the home team. The team struggled at the start of the 2003 season, losing their first three games to the Denver Broncos, the Oakland Raiders, and the Pittsburgh Steelers. But week four brought a win over the Cleveland Browns at 21-14 at Cleveland. And a competitive game against the Buffalo Bills, where the Bengals lost in overtime, helped keep up their spirits. The Bengals won this close game 41-38, against their longtime rivals. (Photograph by Frank Bodie.)

In this huddle picture stands Landon Johnson (No. 59). Johnson graduated from Purdue and was drafted to be a linebacker for the Bengals in 2004. Johnson has played in every game during both the 2004 and 2005 season, including the 2005 Bengals vs. Steelers wild card playoff game. (Photograph by Frank Bodie.)

INTO A NEW HOME

The Beng-Gals cheerleaders cheer before a 2004 Miami vs. Bengals game. There are about 30 Ben-Gals. Missy, a part of the squad, went to the 2006 Pro Bowl to represent the entire Bengals cheerleading team. She also has visited Iceland and the Balkans to dance for the U.S. troops. In March 2003, the Ben-Gals squad went on a European USO tour, making stops at Kosovo and Vienna. More recently, the squad visited the Madigan Army Medical Center on December 17, 2005. (Photograph by Frank Bodie.)

The "Who Dey" Bengals tiger gets the crowd psyched before a 2004 Bengals home game against the Miami Dolphins. The Who Dey term came from the shortened cheer, "Who they think is going to beat them Bengals?" A Cincinnati-based brewery, Hudepohl-Schoenling Brewing Company, also brewed a "Hu-Dey" beer for some time, to join in on the fun. (Photograph by Frank Bodie.)

Members of the military present the colors before a Bengals football game on September 19, 2004. This day, the Bengals beat the Dolphins, 16-13. In the 2004 season, the Bengals started out slow, losing four of their first five games. But they picked things up toward the end, and the team posted a final 8-8 record. (Photograph by Frank Bodie.)

This picture shows Bengals players before they are about to run on the field at the start of a 2004 game against the Miami Dolphins. The three players seen in this picture are Tony Williams (No. 94), Justin Smith (No. 90), and Tory James (No. 20). Williams, a defensive tackle, played for the Bengals from 2001 until 2005. He now plays for the Jacksonville Jaguars. Smith, a defensive end, has played with the Bengals since 2001. He was drafted in the first round and was the fourth overall pick. James, a cornerback, has played for the Denver Broncos (1996–1999) and the Oakland Raiders (2000–2002) before coming to Cincinnati in 2003. He currently plays for the Bengals. (Photograph by Frank Bodie.)

INTO A NEW HOME

Carson Palmer (No. 9) runs onto the field at the start of the 2004 Bengals vs. Dolphins game. Palmer led the Bengals to a noteworthy season in 2003. On November 9, 2003, the Bengals won against the Houston Texans, thanks to Rudi Johnson's 182 rushing yards. Holding a 4-5 record, the Bengals were next scheduled to play the Kansas City Chiefs, who were receiving a lot of attention in the football world for how well they were playing in 2003. The Chiefs' record was 9-0, but that did not stop Bengals wide receiver Chad Johnson from "guaranteeing" a win against the Chiefs. When game day came, the Bengals did not let down their fans. Jon Kitna and Rudi Johnson were the talk of the game; Kitna connected with Peter Warrick for a stunning 77-yard touchdown, and Rudi ran for 165 yards. The Bengals won 24-19. (Photograph by Frank Bodie.)

In 2004, the Bengals continued to solidify their team. Corey Dillon left, and Rudi Johnson (No. 32) was promoted to starting running back. Carson Palmer also got the nod as starting quarterback. Palmer and his team, which most criticized as being too young, lost five of their first seven games. But Palmer soon found his footing, and his arm, as he led the Bengals to a 6-6 record. Palmer suffered a sprained knee in a game against the New England Patriots, who ended up winning 28-35. Unfazed, the Bengals finished with an 8-8 record for the second year in a row. Rudi Johnson finished sixth in the NFL in rushing yards, by posting a gain of 1,454 yards. Bengals fans were once again hopeful for the future. (Photograph by Frank Bodie.)

INTO A NEW HOME

Bengals kicker Shayne Graham (No. 17) attempts to kick a field goal against the Miami Dolphins during the 2004 game. Bengals player Kyle Larson (No. 19) holds the ball steady for Graham. The Bengals played the Dolphins at Paul Brown Stadium on September 19, 2004. More than 65,000 fans showed up to support the team. (Photograph by Frank Bodie.)

This picture was taken during an unusual Bengals Monday night home game against the Denver Broncos. The game, played on October 25, 2004, in Paul Brown stadium, resulted in a win for the Bengals 23-10. The game was broadcast on WCPO—the local ABC television station—and John Madden and Al Michaels called the shots all night. This was the first time in 15 years that the Bengals played a Monday night game. (Photograph by Frank Bodie.)

Chad Johnson joins his teammates before the November 7, 2004, Dallas Cowboys game. As a wide receiver, Johnson has scored 34 touchdowns in his career so far. In 2005, Johnson was recognized for catching a conference-high 97 catches and gaining 1,432 yards. He has been to the Pro Bowl in 2003, 2004, and 2005. Known for being very candid, Johnson is always fun to watch on and off the field. While the Bengals may not have any Super Bowl rings to their name, they have been the testing grounds for many Rookies of the Year. AFL honors went to running back Paul Robinson in 1968 and quarterback Greg Cook and linebacker Bill Bergey in 1969. Offensive Rookies of the Year include two wide receivers, Eddie Brown in 1985 and Carl Pickens in 1992. Offensive Player of the Year went to quarterback Ken Anderson in 1981. NFL MVPs include Anderson (1981) and Boomer Esiason (1988). (Photograph by Frank Bodie.)

INTO A NEW HOME

Chad Johnson holds up Peter Warrick's jersey at the November 7, 2004, Dallas Cowboys game. In 2002, Peter Warrick posted six touchdown catches, the most of any Bengals player that season. He also recorded 53 receptions and ran 606 receiving yards, making him second only to Chad Johnson. In 2001, Warrick posted 70 receptions, giving him a two-season total of 123 receptions. This beat Cris Collinsworth's previous record of 116 in 1981–1982. Both Warrick and Johnson have set team records. Johnson has the most receiving yards per season, for both the 2003 (1,355 yards) and 2004 (1,274 yards) seasons. This beats former record holders Eddie Brown (1988), Tim McGee (1989), and Carl Pickens (1995). Warrick has the second-most average yards per punt return. His 9.7 number just barely falls behind Mike Martin's 9.9 average. Warrick is also on the charts for running two of those punt returns all the way to the end zone for a touchdown. (Photograph by Frank Bodie.)

Carson Palmer practices on the Paul Brown Stadium field at the November 7, 2004, Dallas Cowboys game. Another great Bengals quarterback was Boomer Esiason, who was drafted in 1984 from Maryland. In 1984, Ken Anderson and Boomer Esiason shared the field. Anderson racked up an incredible 2,107 passing yards, and Esiason 530. Anderson was responsible for 10 touchdowns, and Esiason 3. It seems as if the rookie Esiason was being groomed to step into the spotlight; the next year he took over as starting quarterback for the Bengals. (Photograph by Frank Bodie.)

INTO A NEW HOME

Rudi Johnson (No. 32) holds his helmet as he practices before the 2004 game against the Dallas Cowboys. Rudi has a lot more in common with Chad than their last names. Both started with the Cincinnati Bengals in 2001, and both continue to make key plays for the team throughout each season. Rudi is also on the Bengals' all-time records list. He holds the season records for total rushing attempts (361) and the most rushing yards (1,454), both gained during the 2004 season. These numbers beat out former Bengals players Corey Dillon, Pete Johnson, and James Brooks, although all three hold career records. One of Rudi's three best single-game performances for amount of rushing yards is the November 28, 2004, game against the Cleveland Browns. In this game, Rudi rushed for a total of 202 yards. (Photograph by Frank Bodie.)

Levi Jones (No. 76) high-fives Jon Kitna (No. 3) and Odell Thurman (No. 51) as he runs onto the field at the November 7, 2004, Dallas Cowboys game. Jones is a tackle for the Bengals and was drafted in the first round of the 2002 draft. The six-foot-five-inch 307-pound player made key blocking plays during the 2005 season, including the October 30 game against the Green Bay Packers. (Photograph by Frank Bodie.)

T. J. Houshmandzadeh (No. 84) runs out onto the field at the November 7, 2004, Dallas Cowboys game. Another key Bengals player was Ickey Woods. As a rookie in 1988, Woods was also crucial to the Bengals' season that year; he scored 15 touchdowns and ran for 1,066 yards. During this season, Woods trademarked his touchdown dance called "the Ickey Shuffle." (Photograph by Frank Bodie.)

INTO A NEW HOME

The Bengals line up against the Dallas Cowboys in a game at Paul Brown Stadium on November 7, 2004. Carson Palmer (No. 9) takes a hand-off from Rich Braham (No.74). Other members of the offensive team are, from left to right, Jeremi Johnson (No. 31), Tony Stewart (No. 86), Scott Kooistra (No. 75), Bobbie Williams (No. 63), Eric Steinbach (No. 65), and Levi Jones (No. 76). The Bengals went on to win this game by a landslide 26-3. (Photograph by Frank Bodie.)

Chad Johnson (No. 85) prepares to go up against Dallas player Roy Williams (No. 31). Williams was the eighth overall player for the 2002 draft and has played with the Dallas Cowboys ever since. A six-foot 229-pound safety, Williams has gone to the Pro Bowl twice, in 2003 and 2004. Still, the Bengals won this game 26-3. (Photograph by Frank Bodie.)

This picture of the Paul Brown Stadium (specifically the scoreboard) was taken on December 19, 2004. On this date, the Bengals played the Buffalo Bills at home and lost 17-33. The 2004 team split the season with a record of 8-8. (Photograph by Frank Bodie.)

INTO A NEW HOME

Deltha O'Neal (No. 24) waves to the Bengals crowd. O'Neal was born in Palo Alto, California, on January 30, 1977. He attended California College, where he set many school records. In 2000, he was drafted by the Denver Broncos in the first round and was signed July 21 that year. He played for the Broncos until 2003, then was acquired by the Bengals on April 9, 2004. In 2005, O'Neal started in the first 15 Bengals games and won a spot in that year's Pro Bowl. (Photograph by Frank Bodie.)

Carson Palmer (No. 9) and Jeremi Johnson (No. 31) run onto the field before a 2005 game. Johnson was on born September 4, 1980, and played college football for Western Kentucky. He was drafted in 2003 by the Bengals. He scored his first touchdown that same year in a November 9 home game against the Houston Texans, and scored a second touchdown the next week in another home game against the Kansas City Chiefs. (Photograph by Frank Bodie.)

On the left-hand side of this picture are Rudi Johnson (No. 32) and Chad Johnson (No. 85) getting pumped up before a 2005 game. Chad lead the AFC in 2005 for most receptions (97) and most receiving yards (1,432), which won him a trip to the Pro Bowl. Rudi has racked up nine games in which he rushed more than 100 yards, making these two a dynamic duo. (Photograph by Frank Bodie.)

This picture shows Justin Smith (No. 90) during the Bengals vs. Vikings game on September 18, 2005. At six feet four inches and 275 pounds, Smith is the Bengals' defensive end. Smith was drafted by Cincinnati in 2001 during round one of the draft, and he was the fourth pick. Born in Holts Summit, Missouri, Smith played for Missouri before entering the NFL. (Photograph by Frank Bodie.)

INTO A NEW HOME

This picture was taken during the Bengals vs. Vikings game on September 18, 2005. Bengals quarterback Carson Palmer (No. 9) prepares to start a play. The Bengals went on to win this game 37-8. More than 65,000 fans were in attendance. (Photograph by Frank Bodie.)

In this picture, Chad Johnson (No. 85) runs into the end zone, scoring a receiving touchdown. During the 2005 season, Johnson scored nine receiving touchdowns; four were scored during home games, and five were scored on the road. (Photograph by Frank Bodie.)

T. J. Houshmandzadeh (No. 84) practices before the October 30, 2005, game against the Green Bay Packers. Houshmandzadeh started with the Cincinnati Bengals in 2001 when he was drafted in round seven. In 2005, he caught 78 passes and scored eight touchdowns. Houshmandzadeh is well known for playing through the pain; in 2002 he played in every Bengals game, even though he had suffered a groin injury early in the season. He suffered a severe hamstring pull during a preseason game in Indianapolis on August 29, 2003, and then became a starter during the 2004 season. (Photograph by Frank Bodie.)

INTO A NEW HOME

Chris Perry (No. 23) is a Bengals running back drafted by Cincinnati in 2004 in the first round. He continued playing with the Bengals and now has two years of NFL experience under his belt. Perry is active in the community as well as on the field. He started the Chris Perry Foundation, which encouraged young people to do well both in school and in athletics, and Tripping with Perry. This organization is just starting, but his dream is to use it to send underprivileged children on trips nationwide and abroad. (Photograph by Frank Bodie.)

The Cincinnati team runs onto the field at the start of the Packers vs. Bengals game on October 30, 2005. The Bengals do not have a good record against the Green Bay Packers. When the two teams played on September 20, 1998, the Bengals lost 6-13. Also, on the same day in 1992, the Bengals lost an extremely close game to the Packers 23-24. But in 2005, keeping the score close throughout the game, the Bengals won the game in the end 21-14. (Photograph by Frank Bodie.)

Brett Favre (No. 4) prepares to throw to his teammate as the Bengal defense rushes on. Favre spent his first year in the NFL playing with the Atlanta Falcons. But in 1992, he moved to Green Bay, where he continues to be their quarterback. The six-foot-two-inch quarterback went to college at Southern Mississippi and is responsible for more than 400 touchdowns during his career. (Photograph by Frank Bodie.)

INTO A NEW HOME

Toward the end of the second half of the Bengals vs. Packers game, Bengals fan Greg Gall ran onto the playing field and snatched the ball out of Brett Favre's hands as he was preparing to make a throw. Gall was promptly arrested on the field. Gall was charged with criminal trespassing, resisting arrest, and disorderly conduct while intoxicated. He was fined $200, had to perform 230 hours of community service, and was placed on 14 months probation. The incident made the national news and forced officials at Paul Brown Stadium to increase security measures. (Photograph by Frank Bodie.)

The Bengals security guards quickly tackled Greg Gall after his stunt and escorted him off the field. He was arraigned and subsequently visited the Anderson Mercy Hospital to fix an injured back and shoulder from the guards' hit. Gall later denied rumors that he was paid to interrupt play, and apologized profusely for his actions. (Photograph by Frank Bodie.)

CINCINNATI BENGALS HISTORY

Before the January 8, 2006, playoff game against the Steelers, Carson Palmer (No. 9) talks with a reporter as Palmer warms up with Jon Kitna (No. 3) and Chad Johnson (No. 85). In December 2005, Palmer signed a $118.75 million nine-year deal to be the Bengals' quarterback until 2014. This deal makes him one of the highest-paid NFL players in 2006. (Photograph by Frank Bodie.)

In this run onto the field before the Bengals vs. Steelers 2006 playoff game, Bengals quarterback Carson Palmer (No. 9) is seen prominently in the center of the photograph. In front of him run Willie Anderson (No. 71), Rich Braham (No. 74), Eric Steinbach (No. 65), and Bobbie Williams (No. 63). Chris Perry (No. 23) follows behind. (Photograph by Frank Bodie.)

INTO A NEW HOME

The Bengals break their pregame huddle during the Bengals vs. Steelers game. Players in this picture include Tory James (No. 20), Jeremi Johnson (No. 31), Anthony Mitchell (No. 42), Shayne Graham (No. 17), Carson Palmer (No. 9), Chris Henry (No. 15), and Tony Stewart (No. 86). The game started at 4:30 p.m. and was broadcasted on local CBS station Channel 12 WKRC. Tickets for this game went for an average of $92–$250 for lower seat levels, third-level seats, and premium club seats. (Photograph by Frank Bodie.)

This picture was taken at the beginning of the Steelers vs. Bengals playoff game on January 8, 2006. This disappointing end did not deter many Bengals fans. During the season, individual Bengals players reached their personal bests, including Willie Anderson, Shayne Graham, Chad Johnson, Carson Palmer, and Deltha O'Neal, who all played in the Pro Bowl. (Photograph by Frank Bodie.)

In this picture, the Bengals starters are preparing for their big game against the Pittsburgh Steelers in AFC playoffs in January 2006. Standing on the outside of the huddle are Stacy Andrews (No. 79), Eric Ghiaciuc (No. 53), Eric Steinbach (No. 65), and Levi Jones (No. 76). (Photograph by Frank Bodie.)

The Bengals players head onto the field at the start of the Bengals vs. Steelers playoff game. The Pittsburgh Steelers players warm up in the background. After winning this playoff game, the Steelers went on to defeat the Indianapolis Colts and the Denver Broncos in playoff games. Their final Super Bowl match-up was against the Seattle Seahawks. The Steelers won the game 21-10, earning their fifth franchise Super Bowl title. (Photograph by Frank Bodie.)

INTO A NEW HOME

This picture shows the Bengals vs. Steelers playoff game as Bengals quarterback Carson Palmer prepares to make a play. Approximately 65,870 fans showed up to Paul Brown Stadium to watch the playoff games. On just the second offensive play of the game, Carson Palmer threw a 66-yard reception to teammate Chris Henry. As Henry caught the ball and fans cheered, Steelers defensive lineman Kimo von Oelhoffen rolled into Palmer's knee. This hit caused a season-ending knee injury. Oelhoffen plays defensive tackle for the Steelers, but he actually played for the Bengals from 1994 to 1999. (Photograph by Frank Bodie.)

In this picture, a concerned Rudi Johnson (No. 32) looks on as Palmer receives on-field medical attention just seconds after the hit. (Photograph by Frank Bodie.)

Palmer rides off the field after being injured by the Steelers' Kimo von Oelhoffen. The Bengals were still ahead of the Pittsburgh Steelers heading into the third quarter, 17-14. Quarterback Jon Kitna kept the Bengals afloat, but the Steelers, who would go on to win the Super Bowl, proved to be too much. The final score was 17-31. Heading into this game, the Bengals had an 11-5 record. Because of the team's great season, they also hit their highest home season attendance mark, 526,469. (Photograph by Frank Bodie.)

INTO A NEW HOME

4

The Bengal Fanatical:

Fans Through the Decades

Fireworks always accompany the start of a Bengals game. Fans from around the Cincinnati/ Northern Kentucky area tailgate in the surrounding parking lots. They generally eat sausage and sauerkraut and drink Hudepohl beer and orange-and-black Jell-o shots. One couple even got married before the January 2006 playoff game; Jim Reed and Sandy Egnew were married by Steve Hoffman. Cincinnati fans are so important to the team that seven Bengals players—David Pollack, Chad Johnson, Carson Palmer, Rudi Johnson, Willie Anderson, Shayne Graham, and T. J. Houshmandzadeh—all mentioned in a January 4–10, 2006, *Cin Weekly* article, how great the Cincinnati Bengals fans have been during the 2005–2006 season as the team has gotten better and better. (Photograph by Frank Bodie.)

Taken on a sunny day in 2003, September 21, this picture shows the outside of Larry Boberschmidt's van, deemed the Roach. In front stands, from left to right, Jason, L. B., and Tony Boberschmidt. Unfortunately the Bengals went on to lose this home game against the Steelers 10-17. (Courtesy of the Boberschmidt family.)

This picture was taken from the inside of the Roach. Van amenities include stadium seats from the old Cinergy stadium and various other Bengals paraphernalia. Outside the van, L. B. is pointing to the camera. This picture was taken on December 14, 2003, at the Bengals vs. 49ers home game. (Courtesy of the Boberschmidt family.)

THE BENGAL FANATICAL

A boy in the stands shows his Bengals support. This picture was taken during the Bengals vs. Browns home game on December 28, 2003. This game has commonly been nicknamed "the Battle of Ohio." Fans who do not make it to Paul Brown Stadium often invade local bars and restaurants such as Champp's in West Chester, Champions Grille in Price Hill, and Willie's Sports Café in Covington, Kentucky. (Photograph by Frank Bodie.)

This festive Elvis came to tailgate with other fans at the last game of the Bengals' 2003 season. After the parking-lot party, fans went inside Paul Brown Stadium to watch the Bengals play the Browns. Although the Bengals had previously beaten the Browns this season (21-14 at Cleveland), this game proved unsuccessful. The Bengals lost 14-22. (Courtesy of the Boberschmidt family.)

This picture of Jason Boberschmidt and Mick Arnold was taken at the Bengals vs. Browns home game during the 2004 season. The game, played at Paul Brown Stadium on November 28, 2004, was a winning one for the Bengals; they scored 58 to the Browns' 48. (Courtesy of the Boberschmidt family.)

This picture of tailgaters was taken before the November 7, 2004, game against the Dallas Cowboys. The fans in this picture are, from left to right, Yancy Deering, Dan Robke, Tony Boberschmidt, Chris Conway, and Jeff Blom. The Boberschmidt family tailgates in Lot E outside of Paul Brown Stadium. (Courtesy of the Boberschmidt family.)

THE BENGAL FANATICAL

This picture was taken during the Browns home game on December 11, 2005. The Bengals won both their games against the Browns this season; the score was 27-13 when they played in the Cleveland Browns Stadium, and 23-20 when they played in Cincinnati at the Paul Brown Stadium. (Courtesy of the Boberschmidt family.)

The fans in this picture are, from left to right, (first row) Amanda French, an unknown man, and Melissa Sobkowiak; (second row) Brittney Bomar, Nate Jester, Casey Owens, Michael Bodie, Frank Bodie, and Evan Buter. The group tailgates before the November 20, 2005, game against the Indianapolis Colts. (Photograph by Frank Bodie.)

This picture shows fans tailgating before a Bengals home game on the East Plaza at Paul Brown Stadium. After the Bengals' winning 2005 season, the Cincinnati Art Museum commissioned original artwork by famed illustrator and Cincinnati native C. F. Payne to celebrate. The work, titled *Year of the Tiger*, was replicated on posters and sold at the Cincinnati Art Museum and at the January 2006 rally. (Photograph by Frank Bodie.)

This picture shows Bengals fans both young and old. They are, from left to right, Jen Stanley, Steven Kurtz, Pat Kurtz, Brian Stanley, and Matthew "Redman" Kurtz. Pat is the grandmother of these aspiring Who Dey fans. This picture was taken on October 30, 2005, before the Bengals vs. Packers game. (Courtesy of J. Stanley.)

THE BENGAL FANATICAL

This is a picture of the Bengal Bus, which is technically a 1978 Dodge van. John Stanley and his brother, Greg Stanley, bought it after Greg's son, Matt, found it online for sale in Louisville. The bus cost $500, and the Stanley family has added on a little more than $2,000 for upgrades. (Courtesy of J. Stanley.)

This picture shows an entire family of Bengals lovers. They are, from left to right, Brian Stanley, John Stanley, Shelley Stanley, Jeff Stanley, Matt Stanley, Linda Stanley, Dave Stanley, Teri Ludwig, Greg Ludwig, Michelle Stanley, and Greg Stanley. This picture was taken before the Bengals vs. Vikings game on September 18, 2005. (Courtesy of J. Stanley.)

Bengals fans stand in front of the Jungle Express bus, including Lisa McGehey (far left), Bill Stoeckel (No. 2), Jason Clark (No. 80), and Tom McGehey (far right). John Oakley (No. 28) sits in front of the group. The Jungle Express (a 1980 Mini Bird 19-foot bus) was bought by "Bengal Bill" Stoeckel in 2000. The bus cost $1,000 plus another $4,000–$5,000 in repairs, which took about three years to complete. Brendamour and Stoeckel are both owners of the Jungle Express. Stoeckel found the bus sitting in a West Virginia ditch and bought it from the owner of the property it sat on. As Stoeckel was driving it back to his house, it broke down three times. (Courtesy of Bill Stoeckel.)

In this picture Jeff Brendamour, Bill Stoeckel (kneeling), and Jason Clark stand with other Bengals fans. As soon as Stoeckel got the bus home, he painted it orange and knocked out the seats. The inside of the Jungle Express includes artificial turf, built-in coolers, and signatures from Bengals stars such as Marvin Lewis, Anthony Muñoz, and select Ben-Gals cheerleaders. The bus is also equipped with a siren and public address system, as well as couches and bean bags. (Courtesy of Bill Stoeckel.)

　　　　　　　　　　　　　　　THE BENGAL FANATICAL

The Jungle Express bus sits at a recent Marvin Lewis Golf Classic event. The 2005 Marvin Lewis golf classic was held on May 23 at the Shaker Run Golf Club in Lebanon, Ohio. The golf classic pairs up local golfers with Bengals celebrities such as current kicker Shayne Graham and Bengals star alum Anthony Muñoz. (Courtesy of Bill Stoeckel.)

Marvin Lewis stops by the Jungle Express bus to check out some pictures of fans. Jeff Brendamour stands with his back to the camera. Benefits from the golf classic support the Marvin Lewis Community Fund and several other non-profits. The 2006 golf classic took place on May 21, 2006, where more than 200 golfers competed for both prizes and bragging rights. (Courtesy of Bill Stoeckel.)

Cindy and Rich Witterstaetter celebrate before a Bengals game. Cindy's Christmas Bengals hat is especially appropriate, since this picture was taken before the December 24 game between the Bengals and the Buffalo Bills. The Bengals lost this game by a 10-point margin, 27-37. (Courtesy of Rick Witterstaetter.)

Friends tailgate at Longworth Hall with the Cincinnati skyline in the background. The Bengals fans are, from left to right, Larry Wessling, Sarah Simonson, Dave Valerius, and Tony Doyle. This picture was also taken on December 24, 2005. The last regular season game of 2005 was against the Chiefs at Kansas City, where the Bengals lost 3-37. (Courtesy of Rick Witterstaetter.)

THE BENGAL FANATICAL

This loyal fan expressed his Bengal pride by painting his Volkswagen bug with the team's trademark tiger stripes. The vehicle is called the Bengal Bug. Fans who want to take some home team memorabilia with them can order Shayne Graham's Kickin' hot sauce. On sale at area Meijer stores, a portion of the sauce sales benefit Kicks for Kids—a non-profit organization founded by Doug Pelfrey to help at-risk children. (Photograph by Jack Klumpe.)

This picture, taken in front of Paul Brown Stadium, shows the large group of tailgaters in Lot E. Many members of the Bengals team are active in the community; for instance, two Bengals coaches spoke at the 2006 Men's Health Conference. Many players also host community events, such as Madieu Williams's Uncorked Connoisseur Night where guests helped raise money to benefit Williams's charity, which teaches others how to adopt a healthy lifestyle. (Photograph by Frank Bodie.)

David Edwards is the owner of this 1979 Sutphen fire truck dubbed the Bengal Brigade. In this picture stand, from left to right, David, Melissa, Melanie, Madeline, Suzanne, and Pat Edwards. David bought the fire truck eight years ago from the Clearcreek Fire District. He and his father, Pat, painted the truck themselves. (Courtesy of the Edwards family.)

THE BENGAL FANATICAL

Bill Downs and his son, John, bought the 1986 Cadillac hearse in 2004 for $1,400, and spent another $1,400 to have MAACO paint the car orange with black stripes. Bill says he wanted something to show his support for the Bengals that was a bit more out of the ordinary. A mini Bengals helmet is attached to the hearse as a hood ornament. In this picture stand, from left to right, Dean Price, the manager of MAACO; Bill Downs; and John Downs. (Courtesy of Bill Downs.)

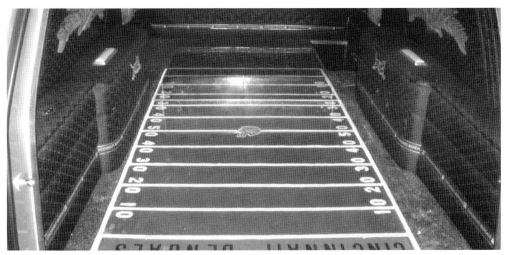

Bill used artificial turf to recreate the inside of Paul Brown Stadium in the back of his hearse. To complete the effect, the window separating the back of the hearse from the front depicts a stadium scene. The official license plate on the back of the hearse is BENGL1. Another feature of the hearse is customized headrests with the Bengals logo. A rubber skeleton holds a Bengals flag. Even the floor mats and steering wheel bear the Bengals insignia. Downs says people often ask him if they can use his hearse after their death to transport their body to the cemetery. (Courtesy of Bill Downs.)

The scoreboard promotes singer Bootsy Collins and his squad before the Bengals vs. Steelers AFC wildcard playoffs in January 2006. The playoff pep rally on Friday, January 6, 2006, gave visitors the chance to sign up for a charity raffle; the winner would get playoff tickets. Cincinnati Bell also provided free ring-tone downloads of the "Fear Da Tiger" cds. (Photograph by Frank Bodie.)

During the January 6th rally, Bootsy Collins signs paraphernalia, including cds, shirts, and posters. Collins produced a song titled "Fear Da Tiger," which was played during the Bengals' spectacular seasons in the 1980s. With the increased interested in the song, and the Bengals themselves, Collins produced the single in 2005 with EO Records. He spent the majority of the January 2006 rally visiting with fans and signing autographs. He also performed his song on stage with some of his friends and the Ben-Gals. (Photograph by Frank Bodie.)

Two police horses, both of which are fully decked out in Bengals gear, watch over the January 2006 rally. The Bengals Playoff Party, on the East Plaza of Paul Brown Stadium, lasted from 6:00 p.m. to 9:00 p.m. and included appearances by Mayor Mark Mallory, various Bengals alumni, Ben-Gals cheerleaders, and the Bengals' mascot. Also, local marching bands provided music. (Photograph by Frank Bodie.)

The rally was held at the stadium, and this shot shows the city of Cincinnati in the background. During 2006, "I'm a Citizen of Bengals Nation" buttons were sold for $2 at various locations around the city including Busken Bakery, Joseph Beth Booksellers, Nicholson's Tavern and Pub, and Jeff Ruby's. (Photograph by Frank Bodie.)

ACROSS AMERICA, PEOPLE ARE DISCOVERING SOMETHING WONDERFUL. *THEIR HERITAGE.*

Arcadia Publishing is the leading local history publisher in the United States. With more than 3,000 titles in print and hundreds of new titles released every year, Arcadia has extensive specialized experience chronicling the history of communities and celebrating America's hidden stories, bringing to life the people, places, and events from the past. To discover the history of other communities across the nation, please visit:

www.arcadiapublishing.com

Customized search tools allow you to find regional history books about the town where you grew up, the cities where your friends and family live, the town where your parents met, or even that retirement spot you've been dreaming about.